D1443945

When Dinosaurs Die

A Guide to Understanding Death

Laurie Krasny Brown and Marc Brown

LITTLE, BROWN AND COMPANY

New York   Boston

All this dying stuff makes me feel sad, worried, and afraid.

In memory of Bob Savage
and to all those who loved him,
especially Beth, Jordan, and Jenna.

Heartfelt thanks for their expert comments and criticism to:
Dorothy Burlage, Ph.D.; Sherry E. Johnson, R.N., Ph.D.; Rabbi Stephen Karcol;
Gerald Koocher, Ph.D.; Monsignor Mimi Pitaro; Reverend Ken Read-Brown;
Beth Savage; Judy Tetreault; and Dr. Mark Vonnegut.

Little, Brown and Company
Hachette Book Group
1290 Avenue of the Americas, New York, NY 10104
Visit our website at www.lb-kids.com

Little, Brown and Company is a division of Hachette Book Group, Inc.
The Little, Brown name and logo are trademarks of Hachette Book Group, Inc.

First Paperback Edition: April 1998
Originally published in hardcover in April 1996 by Little, Brown and Company.

Library of Congress Cataloging-in-Publication Data

Brown, Laurene Krasny.
    When dinosaurs die: a guide to understanding death / Laurie
Krasny Brown and Marc Brown.
        p.   cm.
    Summary: Explains in simple language the feelings people may have
regarding the death of a loved one and the ways to honor the memory of
someone who has died.
    ISBN 978-0316-10917-8 (hc)
    ISBN 978-0316-11955-9 (pb)
1. Children and death—Juvenile literature. 2. Death—Psychological aspects—
Juvenile literature. 3. Bereavement in children—Juvenile literature. [1. Death.] I.
Brown, Marc Tolon.
II. Title.
BF723.D3B77   1996
155.9'37—dc20   95-14511

PB: 20 19 18

SC

Manufactured in China

⟡ CONTENTS ⟡

What Does *Alive* Mean?

Every single living being has a beginning, a time to be alive, and then an ending, or death.

During your lifetime, your body is busy doing its work. You breathe, move, eat, see, hear, touch, taste, smell, grow, talk, play, think, and feel. Yippee! You're alive and a part of the world.

Why Does Someone Die?

Dying is a part of life for every living thing. Death happens for different reasons. Someone may die after a long illness, so everyone knew he or she was going to die.

Other times, it's a complete surprise.

Hurry! Hurry!

Emergency Room

A life can be very long or very short. Even someone just born may not be strong or healthy enough to stay alive.

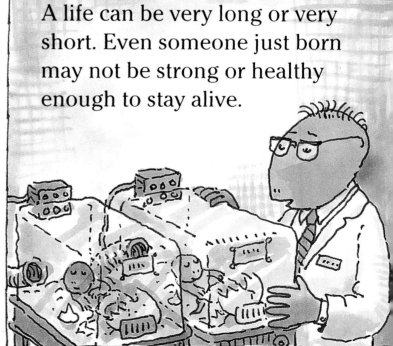

Others may die from being hurt in an accident.
Even when doctors and nurses do everything possible to help,
some accident victims do not recover.

Sometimes lives are lost violently such as when someone kills someone else. It may be in a war…

or for reasons that are very hard to understand, such as poverty, prejudice, and drug abuse.

Someone may even be so upset and without hope about his problems that he kills himself. This is called suicide. All kinds of death make people sad.

Most of us live long, healthy lives. A child, a mother, or father usually lives until he or she is very old.

What Does *Dead* Mean?

When someone dies, her body stops working. The heart stops beating, and breathing stops. The brain doesn't send or receive messages. She no longer can see, hear, touch, taste, smell, eat, play, feel, or think. She cannot move.

Someone dead may look asleep,
but she isn't sleeping and she
cannot wake up.

11

Feelings about Death

When someone you care about dies, you may have all kinds of feelings. It may be hard to believe that a dead relative or friend won't be around anymore.

It's not true. Grandma isn't dead.

She is, too!

In my dream, Yoyo was still alive.

You may have a hard time getting to sleep or have strange dreams or nightmares for a while.

I dreamt a ghost was chasing me and I was running away.

Losing someone who is special to you is *very* hard to understand.

Please, God, let Daddy be alive again. I want him back.

13

It can be very scary when someone close to you dies. You might wonder about how your life will change.

Can we keep our house?

Yes, we can. Try not to worry about that.

You might worry whether you will die, too, or if someone else you love will die.

Will I get sick and die like Cousin Boris?

A healthy kid like you? Not likely.

Things you weren't afraid of before may scare you now.

What if we crash, too?

Well... I will drive very slowly and be extra careful.

15

It's also natural to feel angry when you miss someone so much. Some days you may push away the very hugs you need. There are lots of ways to let out mad feelings without getting in trouble.

Try:
Running
Riding your bike
Swimming
Basketball
Skating
Soccer
Baseball
Punching a pillow
Drawing
Talking to friends

You may want some time to yourself…

and time to be near those you love best.

Some things are worth crying about.

When someone you love dies there is no right or wrong way to feel.

17

Among Friends

When someone in your family dies, your life is likely to be different. But you hope your friends will treat you the same way they did before.

It may be hard for your friends to know what to say or do to help you feel better.

Saying Good-bye

Everyone has to decide how to say good-bye when someone important to him or her dies.

This is a special time to show your love and respect.

21

Friends and family will want to help you honor the life of your friend.
A funeral is a special ceremony for someone who has just died.

No more lettuce for Harriet.

23

Your parents can help you decide whether to attend a funeral. You may have many questions about it.

Going to someone's funeral or memorial service is one way to let a family know you share some of their sadness…and some of their good memories, too.

Is Grandpa's body really in there?

Oh, my! I didn't know Morris Saurus had so many friends.

Even if you don't go to the funeral, you can help out at home, offer extra hugs, or make up a special good-bye poem.

Keeping Customs

There are many special ways of doing things that help us say good-bye to someone who has died.

Some families burn incense and bow low in front of the grave.

Others sing and pray together at the grave. Part of their circle is left open in honor of the dead one's spirit.

Still other families spend several days in mourning by sitting shivah. They sit on a simple wooden bench and light a candle every day.

Some families have the coffin buried underground. Others choose cremation.

Many families continue to honor the dead long after they have died. They may say prayers or prepare a special offering.

What Comes after Death?

Some things about death and dying are very hard to understand, even for grown-ups. No one can know for sure what comes after death, but almost everyone has an opinion about it.

If you have questions about it, ask your family or your religious leader.

Ways to Remember Someone

Even when someone you love dies, you don't lose him completely — you still have your memories. That person can always be a part of you. There are many, many things you can do to remember someone.

Make a scrapbook about her.

Play the game "I remember when..." with your family and friends.

Look at his photograph.

Keep practicing something he taught you.

Write a poem about her.

Keep something of hers in a special place.

Visit her grave.

Name a pet, a doll, or a stuffed animal after him.

Joke about funny things you remember her doing.

Make a new friend who reminds you of her.

Include her in your drawings.

Say a prayer.

Have a picnic to celebrate his birthday.

Plant a tree in his honor.

Isn't being alive awesome?

At other times you may be busy having fun, making friends, learning something new. This is not forgetting the one you love; it just means you're doing other things. Hurray for life!

GLOSSARY

autopsy: careful medical study of a dead body to find out exactly what caused death

cemetery: place for burying the dead; graveyard

coffin: box in which a dead body is buried or cremated

corpse: dead body, usually that of a human being

cremation: the burning to ashes of a dead body

funeral: service, often religious, held to honor the dead at the time of burial or cremation

grave: hole dug in the ground to hold a coffin, usually covered over and marked by a gravestone or other marker

hearse: a special car or other vehicle used to carry the coffin at a funeral

memorial service: service held at any time to honor and remember someone who has died

mourn: to feel or express sadness or grief for a death or other loss

next of kin: closest living relative

wake: a watch over a dead body before burial; a viewing

widow: wife of a person who has died

widower: husband of a person who has died

will: written directions for what is to become of someone's personal property after death